The coach walked in a slow circle a—
Bertha. He studied her from every direc-
tion. He looked her up and down.

"Bertha," said Grizzmeyer at last. *"You are
a girl!"*

"I think he's got it," said one of the cubs.

"Yes, sir!" said Bertha.

"Just what do you think you're doin'?"
growled Grizzmeyer.

"I…I'm going out for the team," she said.

The Berenstain Bears and the Female Fullback

by Stan & Jan Berenstain

A BIG CHAPTER BOOK™

Random House 🏠 New York

Library of Congress Cataloging-in-Publication Data
Berenstain, Stan.
The Berenstain Bears and the female fullback /
by Stan and Jan Berenstain.
      p.   cm. — (A Big chapter book)
SUMMARY: Bothered by the fact that boys and girls are treated
differently in the extracurricular activities at Bear Country School,
Queenie McBear decides to get some changes made.
ISBN 0-679-83611-X (pbk.) — ISBN 0-679-93611-4 (lib. bdg.)
[1. Sex role—Fiction.   2. Schools—Fiction.   3. Football—Fiction
4. Bears—Fiction.]   I. Berenstain, Jan.   II. Title.
III. Series: Berenstain, Stan.   Big chapter book.
PZ7.B4483Bef   1993
[E]—dc20   93-8868

Manufactured in the United States of America   10 9 8 7 6 5 4 3 2 1

BIG CHAPTER BOOKS is a trademark of Berenstain Enterprises, Inc.

Contents

Chapter 1
A Bright New Year

A fine morning mist sifted through the autumn leaves of the Bear family's tree house. Inside, the Bears enjoyed a delicious breakfast of flapjacks with fresh mountain honey. Brother and Sister were full of hopes and plans, for it was the first day of the new school year.

"Guess what!" said Brother. His face glowed with excitement. "I've decided to go out for quarterback on the varsity team this year. And I might run for president of the student body, too."

Papa leaned back in his chair. He beamed with pride. "That's great news," he said. "I've been hoping all summer that you'd go out for quarterback."

Sister added eagerly, "And *I'm* going out for the girls' swim team and the cheerleader squad—"

"Yes sir, that's my boy!" said Papa. "You'll make starting quarterback, I'm sure. And if you run for president, nobody else will have a prayer of winning."

"Didn't you hear what Sister said, Papa?" said Mama in an angry voice. "You know, if she makes the cheerleader squad, she'll be the youngest cub ever to do it."

"Hey, wouldn't that be great," said Papa.
"Then she could cheer when Brother scores
the winning touchdown in the big game
between the Bear Country Cousins and the
Beartown Bullies."

Mama groaned. But Papa went right on talking about Brother and his future on the football team.

This didn't really surprise Mama. For years, she had watched Sister and the other girls get less attention at school than the boys. She had watched them get less support and equipment in sports and other activities. Somehow, it seemed that nearly all the activities outside the classroom were for boys.

This morning, as Mama listened to Papa and Brother ignoring Sister, she knew she had had enough. She knew that Bear Country had a real problem.

What Mama *didn't* know, however, was that a new girl in town would soon cause quite a stir in Bear Country over this very problem.

Chapter 2
A Storm Brewing

Mama Bear wasn't the only one bothered by the difference in how boys and girls were treated at Bear Country School.

"I'd like to go on record right now that I feel some changes must be made," said Queenie McBear. A group of girl cubs had gathered around her in front of the school. They were waiting for the bell to ring.

"Like what?" asked Sister.

"I'll tell you like what," said Queenie. "Like how many years in a row has a boy been student body president and a girl been vice president?"

"As far back as I can remember," answered Sister.

"Right," said Queenie. "And who has all the fun and excitement of football, with cheerleaders and the band and packed grandstands?"

"The *boys*," said Babs with a frown.

"Right. And who has field hockey with no cheerleaders and no band and empty grandstands?"

"Us," said Lizzy.

"Right," said Queenie. "Now I ask you: Is that fair?"

"No!" cried all the girls at once.

"You're darn right it's not!" said Queenie.

"And this year Yours Truly is going to do something about it. I'm running for student body president. *And* I have a few ideas about the girls' sports program!"

Everything Queenie had said seemed to be true. But some cubs didn't feel they should vote for her just because she was a girl or just because she believed in girls' rights.

Some were thinking of voting for Brother even though he was a boy. A few, in fact, were planning to vote for Brother because he was a boy. "I think he's cute," one of them said with a giggle.

"If *that's* the way you feel," growled Queenie, "maybe you deserve him."

"You're right, Queenie," said Sister. She was still upset over what Papa had said at breakfast that morning. She turned to the other girls. "There's something I've been wondering about for a long time," she said. "The boys' football team has girl cheerleaders. So why doesn't the girls' hockey team have *boy* cheerleaders?"

"Right on!" cried Queenie as she gave Sister and Lizzy high-fives.

The school bell rang. As the girls filed into the main corridor, they saw Brother Bear, Cousin Freddy, and a lot of the other boys crowded around the bulletin board by the principal's office. They were signing up

for football and other activities. Nearby, the
school trophy case gleamed with dozens of
trophies won by the boys' sports teams. In
one corner of the case sat a few small trophies won by girls' teams.

"Just look at that," said Queenie. She
turned to her friends with a sneer. "Some
serious changes have to be made around
here. *For sure.*"

Chapter 3
Broom and the Bullhorn

A few days later, Brother Bear and Cousin Freddy went to football tryouts at the school athletic field. As usual, the tryouts

were run by Coach "Bullhorn" Grizzmeyer. He was also the assistant principal and disciplinarian of Bear Country School. He was nicknamed "Bullhorn" because he didn't need one.

Just before tryouts started, Coach Grizzmeyer went over the sign-up sheet with Cousin Freddy, the team manager. Meanwhile, Brother, Too-Tall Grizzly, and the other candidates for the team warmed

up. They tossed footballs back and forth and charged out of their three-point stances.

The grandstand was empty except for someone who sat alone—someone whom no one had noticed.

Coach Grizzmeyer looked down at his watch and yelled, "All right! Let's get this season under way! I want all you guys trying out for offensive line and blocking back to move over here to the blocking frame!"

The blocking frame was very heavy and difficult to move. The coach rode on the back of it to make it heavier still.

Cousin Freddy checked the name at the top of the sign-up sheet. "Barry Bruin!" he called out.

Lizzy's brother was a big cub who had his heart set on playing offensive tackle. He took up his stance and charged the frame.

He hit the padding with a WHACK and jarred it. But he failed to budge it.

"Ready when you are," teased the coach. The other cubs laughed. "Just kidding, son. Don't worry. You'll get another chance. Next!"

Freddy called out each name in turn, and the cubs hurled themselves at the heavy frame. Only Too-Tall managed to move it more than a few feet.

Soon it seemed everyone had had a turn. But there was one more name at the bottom of the list. And Freddy didn't recognize it. "B. Broom?" he finally called out.

The cubs looked at each other with raised eyebrows. No one recognized the name. Brother turned to Barry Bruin. "Must be a new cub in town," he said. "Do you know him?" Barry shook his head.

Coach Grizzmeyer looked around at all

the cubs. "B. Broom!" he roared at the top of his lungs. "If you want your turn, you'd better come quick!"

The mysterious B. Broom, it seemed, hadn't heard Cousin Freddy's rather weak call. On the other hand, Coach Grizzmeyer's famous bellow could be heard clearly everywhere on the school grounds. The moment it rang out across the playing field, the lone figure high in the stands stood up and hurried down to the field.

"Present, Coach!" shouted the big, strong-looking candidate.

Everyone stared. Coach Grizzmeyer looked down over his glasses at the powerfully built cub. "Are you Broom?" he asked, frowning.

"Yes, sir!" said the cub.

The coach played nervously with the whistle hanging from his neck. "But you're wearing earrings," he said. There was some snickering from the players.

"Yes, sir."

"And a hairbow—two hairbows, in fact."

"Yes, sir."

From the sidelines came a loud whisper: "Hey, Coach can count."

"Cool it!" barked Grizzmeyer. He turned back to the would-be football player. "Says here 'B. Broom.' What's the 'B' stand for?"

"Bertha, sir."

The coach walked in a slow circle around Bertha. He studied her from every direction. He looked her up and down. He put his hand to his chin as if in deep thought. There was more snickering from the players.

"Bertha," said Grizzmeyer at last. *"You are a girl!"*

"I think he's got it," said one of the cubs.

"Yes, sir!" said Bertha.

Bertha was indeed a girl—a *big* girl. She was bigger, in fact, than any of the boys except Too-Tall Grizzly. But she had a soft, round baby face. And right now that face looked very worried.

BERTHA, <u>YOU</u> <u>ARE</u> <u>A</u> <u>GIRL</u>!

"Just what do you think you're doin'?" growled Grizzmeyer.

That made Bertha look even more worried. She felt her knees go a little wobbly. "I...I'm going out for the team," she said. "I know the game real well, Coach. I've played lots of football with my brothers—"

"With your brothers?!" yelled Grizzmeyer. "This isn't some backyard family fun game I'm running here, Broom! This is varsity football—*boys'* varsity football! You're way out of bounds, young lady! Football's a *boys'* game. It always has been and it always will be. And as long as I have enough breath in me to blow this whistle, there will be no girls on any football team coached by Yours Truly, Mervyn 'Bullhorn' Grizzmeyer! You got that, Broom? Now get off the field and stop holding up my practice!"

Bertha's lower lip trembled as she fought back tears. "But, Coach—" she said. "Aren't you even going to see what I can do?"

"Off the field!" boomed the coach. "Manager, line 'em up for another round of blocking!"

At that moment you could have heard a daisy petal fall in the wide open space of the practice field. Even the cheerleader practice had stopped. All eyes were fixed on Bertha.

Chin on chest and heart breaking, Bertha Broom walked slowly off the field. The only sound was the mocking laughter of Too-Tall and his gang.

"Shut up, Too-Tall," snarled the coach. "Let's get on with it."

Chapter 4
Fuel for the Fire

Next, Coach Grizzmeyer had the cubs do ten minutes of exercises. As Brother Bear pedaled the air, feet high, he saw Bertha Broom leaving the playing field.

"That's a shame," he said to Barry Bruin, who was pedaling beside him. "Coach was kind of hard on her."

"Yeah," Barry grunted from under the weight of his heavy legs. "But what's Coach supposed to do? Girls can't play football. They're just not tough enough."

"I guess you're right," said Brother. "But did he have to be so nasty about it?"

"And they don't have the endur—" Barry broke off, already out of breath.

"Endurance?" said Brother. He went back to concentrating on his pedaling. He wasn't at all sure how he felt about what had just happened.

But the same could not be said for the cheerleaders. They crowded around Bertha.

"That was really mean of Coach," said Lizzy Bruin. She gave Bertha a friendly pat on the back.

"Yeah," said Sister. "He could have let you try out, at least."

"It just goes to show you, girls," said Queenie. "Our famous coach is nothing more than a big old male chauvinist pig! And so are all those boys out there. Not one of them stood up for Bertha's right to try out!"

"I think it was really brave of you to go out for football," said Babs Bruno to Bertha. "What made you do it?"

But Bertha was too upset to talk. The tears she had held back in front of the boys now burst forth in full flood.

With kind words and encouragement, the cubs walked her to the girls' locker room.

Chapter 5
A House Divided

Bertha Broom was not only the first girl ever to show up at Coach Grizzmeyer's football tryouts. She was also the first boy or girl ever to be turned down for a tryout. Coach Grizzmeyer's treatment of Bertha Broom had all the makings of one of the biggest news events ever in Bear Country.

And everyone knew that that could lead to big trouble. Which is just what happened.

As quickly as you could say "women's rights," Bear Country was up in arms. Half of the citizens—mostly males, but some females—were shocked and angry that a girl would even *think* of trying out for football, much less do it. The other half were just as shocked and angry that a girl hadn't even been given a chance to try out for the team.

The argument reached right down into families. Family members began warring with one another, usually male against female. It seemed to reach every family in Bear Country. Even the Bear family, who got along so well with each other most of the time, began to fight.

A few days after the tryouts, Papa Bear sat in the living room reading the *Bear*

LISTEN TO THIS!

Country Intelligencer. Already the newspaper was full of articles and letters about Bertha and the tryouts.

"Hey," Papa called to Mama. She was in the kitchen fixing the cubs an after-school snack. "Here's a letter from Farmer Ben. Listen to this: 'And as for Miss Bertha Broom, anyone who did what she did must be a troublemaker. Why else would a girl butt in where she doesn't belong?' "

"And do you agree with that?" Mama called from the kitchen.

Papa laid the newspaper down across his lap and thought. "Hmm," he finally said. "No, I don't."

"Oh?" Mama said hopefully. "I'm a bit surprised to hear that. Why not?"

"Well, Bertha might not mean any harm at all," said Papa. "She might just be confused about how girls should act."

Mama groaned and stalked into the living room. "Oh, you're *so* understanding, Papa Bear," she said. "Have you thought of a third possibility?"

Papa frowned and scratched his head. "Third possibility? What could that be?"

"That Bertha Broom just *likes to play football*," said Mama.

"Ha!" said Papa. "That's no reason for her to try out for the *boys'* football team!"

"Oh, no?" said Mama. "What do you think she should do: try out for the *girls'* football team?"

"Of course not! There *isn't* any girls'—" Papa broke off. He suddenly saw the point Mama was trying to make. "Er...uh...now wait a minute," he said. "You're twisting my thoughts around...."

The front door opened, and Brother and Sister came in for their snack. But Mama

and Papa were so busy arguing that they didn't even notice the cubs. Brother and Sister stood quietly watching and listening.

"You don't need *me* to twist your thoughts around," Mama teased. "You do a fine job of it yourself."

"Very funny," said Papa. "I'll bet these other letters agree with *me*." He picked up the newspaper again. "Here's the next one: 'Anyone who calls Bertha Broom a trouble-maker should think again. Maybe she just likes to play football....'" Papa's voice trailed off.

"Exactly!" cried Mama. "Who wrote that fine, intelligent letter?"

"Hmm," said Papa. "This letter is signed...*Mrs.* Ben. Well, what would you expect from a female?" Mama was about to answer when Brother cleared his throat loudly.

"Oh, hi, cubs," said Mama. "Er...your snacks are all ready in the kitchen."

But the cubs didn't move. "What were you two arguing about?" asked Sister. "Bertha Broom?"

We weren't arguing," said Mama. "We were just...*discussing.*"

"It sounded like arguing to me," said Brother.

"Me too," said Sister.

Mama sighed. "The cubs are right, dear," she said. "Your papa and I *were* discussing Bertha Broom. And perhaps we were arguing just a bit."

Papa smiled and put his arm around Mama's shoulders. "But remember, cubs, your mama and I never argue about anything *important*," he said.

"Do you mean to say," said Mama, "that women's rights are not important?"

"Sure, they're important," said Papa. "But what do women's rights have to do with some silly girl going out for the boys' football team?"

"They have *everything* to do with it!" shouted Mama. "And furthermore…"

The Bear family wasn't the only family discussing the football fate of Bertha Broom. Farmer and Mrs. Ben were discussing it so loudly they frightened their cows. Squire and Mrs. Grizzly got so angry they began throwing things. All was quiet at the Bruins. But that was because Mr. and Mrs. Bruin had gotten so angry they had stopped speaking to each other.

There was no question about it: The Bertha Broom story was spreading through Bear Country like wildfire.

Chapter 6
A Clean Bill of Health

Over the next few days, nearly all of Bear Country's families were arguing about Bertha Broom and the tryouts. But fortunately, their arguments weren't getting in the way of their deep-down love and caring for each other.

Still, most of them knew that the question of girls' rights to play sports was very important. They knew that it couldn't be ignored. Groups formed to pressure the school and the Bear Country government to decide whether or not Bertha Broom should be allowed to try out for football.

One evening after dinner, the Bear family was relaxing in the living room watching the news on TV when the doorbell rang. Papa got up to answer it. There stood Queenie McBear and her mother. Each held a clipboard and a pen.

"Good evening, Papa," said Mrs. McBear pleasantly. "Haven't seen you in a while. How have you been?"

"Oh, just fine," said Papa. He pointed to the TV set, which was chattering away about you-know-what. "Like everyone else around here, we're all wrapped up in this Bertha Broom business. Would you like to come in and watch with us?"

"Thank you, Papa, but we can't stay," said

Mrs. McBear. "It's the Bertha Broom business that brings us here. You see, I have a petition here. It asks the Bear Country Council to pass a law allowing girls to play on the sports teams at Bear Country School."

Papa's eyes narrowed. "As I see it," he said, "girls are *already* allowed to play on the Bear Country School teams. For example, they play on the girls' hockey and girls' volleyball teams."

Brother whispered to Sister, "Here we go again."

Mama came forward. "*You* know what she means, Papa. I'd be glad to sign, Mrs. McBear. And if there's anything else I can do to help…"

Sister came to the door. "Have you got a petition, too?" she asked Queenie.

"You bet," said Queenie. "For a cheerleader strike!"

ALL RIGHT!

"All right!" cried Sister, high-fiving with Queenie.

"Cheerleader strike?" said Papa. "You can't be serious! Next, I suppose one of you girls will want to run for student body president against Brother just because he's a boy."

Queenie looked slyly up at Papa. "I thought you already knew about that," she said.

"You mean, you *are* running?" gasped Papa.

"And I'm going to beat the pants off him, too!" said Queenie.

"That does it!" yelled Papa. He was barely able to catch his breath. "I think you two had better go bother someone else with your petitions!"

Brother rushed to the door to try to smooth things over. He was grateful to Papa for sticking up for him, but he didn't like the way Papa was going about it. "Bear Country is a democracy. So Queenie has every right to run. You remember democracy, Papa. After all, it was you and Mama who taught me about it."

Papa calmed down. "Well...I...er... You're right, Brother. Guess I got a little carried away there. Didn't mean to be rude. I'm just so upset about this Bertha Broom business...."

"That's quite all right, Papa," said Mrs. McBear. "I suppose we've all been a bit touchy lately."

"You can say that again," said Papa. "Why, the very idea of girls playing on the Bear Country football team..."

"In the first place," said Queenie, "it's not 'girls.' It's one girl. And in the second place, all she wants is a chance to try out for the team."

"And in the third place," shouted Papa, "the whole idea is crazy!" He raged on. "Girls playing football! Whoever heard of such nonsense? Why, girls aren't tough enough. They're just not medically fit to play football!"

Mrs. McBear pointed past Papa to the TV screen. "Speaking of 'medically fit,'" she said, "isn't that Dr. Gert Grizzly?"

"What's she doing on TV?" asked Mama.

Everyone crowded around the TV set. Bear Country's roving reporter, Wally Bearloo, was speaking.

"As we said earlier, Mayor Honeypot has asked Bear Country's medical expert, Dr. Gert Grizzly, to examine Bertha Broom to

see if she is medically fit to play football. Dr. Grizzly finished her examination a few hours ago.

"And what are your findings, Doctor? Is Bertha Broom medically fit for football?" asked Wally.

Dr. Grizzly looked straight into the cam-

era and smiled. "After a thorough examination of Bertha Broom," she said, "I find that she is medically fit not only for football but also for wrestling and rugby. And she's probably fit for running through brick walls as well."

"Yahoo!" cried Queenie and Sister. This

time even Mama and Mrs. McBear joined the girls in their high-fives.

"Humph!" snorted Papa. He stomped up the stairs to the bedroom. "What does Gert Grizzly know about football! She wouldn't know a quarterback sack from a potato sack!"

Queenie and her mother rushed off. They wanted to continue their door-to-door campaign while Dr. Grizzly's announcement was still hot.

When the TV news was over, Sister went upstairs to do her homework. That left Mama and Brother in front of the TV. But neither of them was watching. They had other things on their minds. Especially Brother.

"Don't you have homework, too?" Mama asked.

Brother shrugged. "Yeah," he said. But he made no move toward the stairs.

Mama could tell that something was bothering Brother. And she had a pretty good idea what it was. "How about helping me with the dishes first," she said.

"Okay," said Brother. He followed Mama into the kitchen.

Brother picked up a dish towel and stood
beside Mama at the sink. "So, how has football practice been going?" Mama asked. She
handed Brother the first dish to be dried.

Brother sighed. "I'm not really sure," he
answered. "All the screaming and yelling is
really getting to us."

"Screaming and yelling?" said Mama.

"From the Jeerleaders."

"Jeerleaders? I don't understand," said Mama.

"Yeah," said Brother. "A bunch of girls formed a group called the 'Jeerleaders.' They come out to every practice with megaphones and jeer us instead of cheer us. And

now the *real* cheerleaders are going on strike." Brother shook his head sadly. "We won't have much of a season if this keeps up."

Mama shook her head too. "I certainly hope all this can get worked out before the big Bear Country–Beartown game. But I've been wondering. How would you feel if Bertha Broom *did* wind up on the team?"

"That's just it," Brother said. "I don't think I'd mind—not if she was really good enough to play. The more I think about the whole thing, the more I remember that awful look on Bertha's face when the coach bawled her out and sent her packing. It might take a little while, but I'll bet the guys could get used to her being on the team."

"As the starting quarterback, your opinion should carry some weight in the locker room," said Mama. "What would happen if you told the team how you felt?"

Brother rolled his eyes. "They'd just make fun of me. They'd call me a 'girl-lover' and stuff like that. Except for the ones who'd call me a 'traitor,' that is. Most of them are real stubborn about this, like Papa. If there were just some other way to get them to let Bertha try out..."

Mama looked down at Brother with a twinkle in her eye. "But you just said it yourself a minute ago!"

"What?" asked Brother.

"That the Bertha Broom problem is wrecking the whole season. If you pointed that out to your teammates and the coach..." Mama let her voice trail off to give Brother a chance to finish the thought.

Suddenly Brother's eyes grew wide. "...then maybe they would let her try out

just to get it all over with!" he exclaimed.
"None of them think she can make the
team, anyway. So they might go for it!"

"Good idea," said Mama.

"Yeah! Glad I thought of it!" Brother
cried. And he raced to the phone to call
Cousin Freddy.

Chapter 7
A Tale of Two Locker Rooms

The next afternoon Brother and Freddy met with the team in the boys' locker room before practice.

"You see," said Brother to the team, "this problem with Bertha Broom is wrecking the whole season for everyone. Why don't we just let her try out, and be done with it?"

The room was silent. Most of the players looked over at Coach Grizzmeyer. They waited to see what he would say.

But it was not Coach Grizzmeyer who spoke first. It was Too-Tall. "I think it's a great idea," he said. "There's no downside to it. That's because we all know that Bertha

doesn't stand a chance of making the team. But there is a definite upside to it. We can teach that uppity, trouble-making girl a real lesson." He winked at Skuzz, his right-hand man in the gang. "We'll give her teeth such a rattling, she won't be able to spell football, much less play it!"

The truth was that the position Bertha wanted to try out for was fullback. That was Too-Tall's position, so he *really* had it in for her.

Too-Tall sat down. All eyes turned to Coach Grizzmeyer. He stood leaning against the locker-room wall with his arms folded across his chest. With his brow knitted in thought, he stood that way for quite a while.

"All right," he said at last. "We'll give the Broom kid a tryout tomorrow afternoon. Then maybe we'll get some peace and quiet around here. Freddy, you run out there right now and tell those so-called 'Jeerleaders' to pack up their pompoms and go home."

"Right, Coach!" Freddy said, and dashed out the door.

Now Coach Grizzmeyer lowered his voice. "And as for rattling teeth and any other rough stuff," he said, "I don't want to see any blood or broken bones. But I wouldn't object to a few well-placed bruises.

Somebody's got to teach these girls who think they want to play football that it's not hopscotch, jacks, or tiddlywinks. And what I just said is between me and you and the locker-room walls. Understand? Okay, let's go. It's practice time!"

The news that Coach Grizzmeyer would let Bertha try out spread quickly. The cheerleaders called off their strike that very afternoon and scheduled a practice right away.

While the team was out on the playing field, the cheerleaders gathered in their locker room to change into their outfits. The mood in the locker room was joyous. Queenie McBear was especially excited. She believed that the coach's decision was partly due to her women's rights campaign for president.

"Listen up, girls," Queenie said as she

zipped up her skirt. "We can't stop now just because we won a tryout for Bertha. When Bertha makes the team, we have to fill the grandstand with girls."

"Don't you mean *if* she makes the team?" said Lizzy.

"No, I don't," said Queenie. "Bertha *has* to make the team. She has to do it for the cause of women's rights!"

"We should make up some brand-new cheers for Bertha," suggested Sister.

"And you should lead every cheer tomorrow, Queenie," added Lizzy Bruin. "You'll pick up some extra votes that way."

Suddenly the girls noticed someone

standing at the locker-room door. It was
Bertha Broom. She was dressed in blue
jeans and a green football jersey.

"Hey, Bertha!" shouted Queenie. She
jumped to her feet. "Congratulations!" All
the cheerleaders joined in: "Hip, hip,
hooray! Hip, hip, hooray! Hip, hip, hooray!"

Bertha blushed and looked down at the ground. "Speech!" called Sister. "Speech!" yelled the other girls.

Still blushing, Bertha looked up. "I really appreciate your support," she said softly. She turned to Queenie. "And I know how badly you want to be president. But I wish you wouldn't make such a fuss. I just want a chance to play football. That's all."

"We know you do," said Queenie. She looked around at her fellow cheerleaders. "And as a candidate for president of the student body, I'm making it my job to see you *get that chance!*"

"Right on!" shouted the cubs.

"Now come on, girls!" Queenie said. "Let's get to work on our Bertha Broom cheers!"

The cheerleaders swept through the locker-room door. They left Bertha standing alone, staring after them. "Awful nice of them," she said to herself. "But I don't really *need* any help making the team."

Chapter 8
The Fateful Tryout

Despite Bertha's wishes, the next afternoon
the Bear Country School grandstand was
filled with girls. Some held hand-painted
signs reading "Go Bertha!," "Bertha Broom
Can't Be Bullied!," and "Sweep Too-Tall
Out of a Job!" On the sidelines, the cheerleaders led the roar of the crowd: "Give me
a 'B'! Give me an 'R'! Give me an 'O'! Give
me an 'O'!..."

Coach Grizzmeyer climbed onto the
blocking frame and raised his bullhorn

voice above the noise. "Okay, Broom! First test: blocking!" He reached down and cranked the frame's brake handle as far as possible. "Okay, dearie, let 'er rip!"

At the sound of Grizzmeyer's whistle, Bertha came charging like a locomotive and slammed into the blocking frame with a loud THWACK! Coach Grizzmeyer hung on for dear life as he was carried a good fifteen yards downfield. "Stop! Stop! Okay! Okay!" he yelled.

A big cheer went up from the stands. "Yay, Bertha! Yay, Bertha! Y-a-a-a-a-y, Bertha!" screamed the cheerleaders.

The next phase of the tryout was a scrimmage. "Anybody can run into a blocking frame, Miss Broom," said Grizzmeyer. "The real question is, can you play the game of football? Since we've already got a fullback, let's see you play linebacker on defense. Your job is to get to the quarterback." He gave a little chuckle and winked at Brother.

Bertha took up her position behind the defensive line as the offensive squad huddled. Brother called a short pass play to Skuzz.

"Don't worry about Miss Featherduster," said Too-Tall. "I'm gonna flatten her with my own personal slobber-knocker block."

"She'll never know what hit her!" added Skuzz.

Skuzz was right. Bertha never knew what hit her. Because nothing hit her. Bertha was as quick as she was powerful. She cleverly sidestepped Too-Tall's block. Then she sacked Brother for a bone-jarring loss.

"Sorry about that," she told Brother as she helped him to his feet and dusted him off.

Back in the huddle, Too-Tall growled, "Beginner's luck. Give me the ball this time. I'm going right up the middle and knock her on her tail!"

But the second play from scrimmage ended up looking a lot like the first. Fullback Too-Tall took the hand-off from Brother and charged right at Bertha through a big hole in the line. Before Too-Tall knew what had hit him, his helmet smashed into Bertha's right shoulder pad. Too-Tall went flying backward and landed smack on his backside. He sat up, blinking at his powerful tackler.

"You okay?" Bertha asked. She really was concerned about him.

"Of course, I'm okay!" said Too-Tall. "I

slipped on a wet spot, that's all!"

On the sidelines, the cheerleaders rode make-believe motorcycles. "*Vroom! Vroom! Bertha Broom!*" they yelled.

For the third play, Brother called a crossing pattern. But Bertha read the play perfectly. She intercepted his pass near midfield and headed for the end zone like a stampeding buffalo. One after another,

tacklers bounced off her like rag dolls. As she reached the goal line, Bertha sent Barry Bruin sprawling with a straight-arm.

The fans went wild as the coach smiled from the sidelines. If there was one thing Mervyn "Bullhorn" Grizzmeyer believed in more than male chauvinism, it was football. And he was already starting to see Bertha Broom not as a *girl* but as a *football player.* A *winning* football player.

Chapter 9
The Campaign Thickens

With Bertha Broom's great tryout success, Queenie McBear's campaign for president took on speed. Sister Bear and Lizzy Bruin organized a group called Girls for Queenie. In the final days before the election, the group held rallies and marches on the school grounds. So did Boys for Brother, the group from the other side.

Queenie gave lively speeches about the need for change at Bear Country School. Brother's speeches were not as lively as Queenie's. The truth was that they were a little dull. That may have been because Brother didn't really mind if girls wanted to play football and other "male" sports. In fact, he was a bit surprised by the strong feelings that everyone seemed to have about it.

At the same time, Brother was getting less and less excited about being elected president. Winning would be fun, of course.

But he wondered if he really wanted to take on such a big job. Being the starting quarterback for the Bear Country Cousins was taking up a lot of time and energy. Not only were there daily practices and locker-room meetings, but every night before bed Brother had to study the playbook. And this was all on top of schoolwork and home chores. Brother was beginning to feel that he had already taken on all he could handle.

Brother secretly wished he could back out of the whole election. But he knew it was too late. If he backed out at the last minute, Queenie would surely win. And the boys of Bear Country School would probably never forgive him—even if he led the Bear Country Cousins to a championship.

Brother was beginning to think that maybe the team really *would* win a championship. Most of the boys were already getting used to Bertha Broom being on the team. And Bertha was so good at running the football that Coach Grizzmeyer decided to make her fullback and move Too-Tall to tight end.

"You've gotta be kidding!" growled Too-Tall when he heard the news. "Little Miss Hairbows, a fullback? What if she loses an earring?"

But the truth was that Too-Tall's height

made him a natural pass-catching end. Everyone hoped he would settle into his new position.

With Bertha blocking for Brother on pass plays, the offense really began to come together. And none too soon, because the first game of the season would be the toughest. The Bear Country Cousins were playing last year's champions, the Beartown Bullies.

The day before the election and two days before the big game, Sister Bear and Lizzy Bruin made a careful head count of cubs in the school. They found that there was an even number of girls and boys—fifty-six of each.

"Wait till Queenie hears this," said Sister. "She thought if she got every girl's vote, she would win for sure. She never thought it could be a tie. But now it looks as if she has to go after the *boys,* too."

Sister and Lizzy ran straight to Queenie's house to tell her the news. Queenie smiled a knowing smile and said, "You just leave that little matter to me."

When Sister got home, she told Brother the news that there could be a tie. He just shrugged and said nothing. His mind was on the big game.

Chapter 10
The Big Game

Mr. Honeycomb, the school principal, decided not to announce who had won the election until the end of the big game. That was fine with Brother. After all, he needed to keep his mind on one thing and one thing only—beating the Beartown Bullies.

On game day, Brother Bear was not the only one thinking about football. With the

election over, it seemed as though everybody in Bear Country had just one thing on their minds—football.

The grandstand filled to overflowing. The whole field was ringed with cheering fans. The noise was deafening. Cheerleaders from each school were shouting their cheers at the same time. Each band boomed out its own fight song.

Finally, above the noise, the voice of Bert Brunowski, the game's announcer, could be heard.

"...and now, your very own Bear Country Cousins! Starting at quarterback...Brother Bear. At tight end...Too-Tall Grizzly. At fullback...Bertha Broom...," he blared.

The Bear Country Cousins were ready to take the field when Coach Grizzmeyer realized that someone was missing. "Hey, where's Bertha?" he yelled. He looked frantically around. Everyone began looking this way and that.

"Here she comes," said Brother, pointing toward the girls' locker room. "I guess she was a little late getting her gear on...Hey, wait a minute...." Brother couldn't believe his eyes. "She doesn't *have* her gear on!"

Bertha walked over to the sidelines. She

was wearing her helmet. But she had on an
ordinary sweatsuit—and no pads! She held
out a blue-and-gold piece of material tied
into knots. It was a Bear Country Cousins
uniform!

"Coach!" moaned Bertha. "Somebody sneaked into the locker room and did this! And they stole my pads, too!"

Coach Grizzmeyer glared down at the knotted uniform. His face turned bright red with anger. "Must have been some rotten male chauvinist pig!" he roared. "Why, if I ever get my hands on the joker who—"

The coach suddenly stopped speaking and looked over at Too-Tall. "Anyone here know anything about this?" he snarled.

All eyes, even Skuzz's, turned on Too-Tall. The same thought crossed everyone's mind. They all knew that Too-Tall was angry at Bertha. After all, he had been fullback until she came along. But was he so angry that he would wreck the big game and ruin the whole season?

Then, as everyone stared, something unbelievable happened. Too-Tall took off his own shoulder pads and handed them to Bertha. "Our best blocker and ball-carrier needs these more than I do," he said. "Besides, I can reach for passes better without 'em." A shocked murmur ran through the team.

Meanwhile, Freddy untied the last knot in Bertha's uniform. Within minutes, Bertha was dressed and ready to play. Loud cheers rang out as the Bear Country Cousins took the field.

High in the stands, Papa Bear jumped to his feet and yelled, "We're gonna make 'em look silly! We're gonna destroy 'em!"

Even Mama, who didn't know much about football, joined in. "Throw a field goal, Brother! Throw a field goal!" she yelled.

As usual, Papa was letting himself get a bit carried away in the heat of the moment. The Beartown Bullies were no pushovers. They were a tough, skilled, well-coached football team. And that afternoon, they played like the champions they were.

They scored first on a long pass that went forty yards in the air. And they scored again

early in the second quarter on a field goal.

With the clock running down at the close of the first half, Brother hit Too-Tall with a long pass up the middle. Bertha finished the drive with a hard-hitting ten-yard carry into the end zone.

The crowd went wild! But at halftime, the Cousins were still trailing ten to seven....

The two teams played to a standstill

through the third quarter and most of the fourth. Finally, with only twelve seconds to go, the Cousins had the ball on their own thirty-yard line.

There was time for just one more play. A field goal would tie it. But the Cousins weren't close enough to even try for one. It would have to be a touchdown or nothing.

Brother sensed that the Bullies expected a long pass to Too-Tall. So he called a trick play in the huddle.

At the snap, Too-Tall broke downfield and angled toward the far sideline. The whole defensive backfield followed him. Then Brother faked a hand-off to Skuzz. This drew the defensive line and linebackers to the same side of the field. Next Brother faked a bomb to Too-Tall downfield. Then he tucked the ball under his arm and headed for the opposite sideline.

With Bertha blocking for him like a Sherman tank, Brother raced down the sideline toward the end zone. As the final second ticked off the scoreboard clock, he danced over the goal line and spiked the ball behind his back. The crowd roared like thunder.

Through the cheers of the crowd came a voice over the loudspeakers: "Final score: Bear Country Cousins, thirteen. Beartown Bullies, ten!"

Down on the field, the Bear Country Cousins tried to lift Coach Grizzmeyer to their shoulders. But they didn't have enough strength until Bertha Broom moved in with her mighty shoulders. Proudly, they carried the coach off the field.

In the stands, Papa was wildly cheering his son's play. But then suddenly he started shouting, "Bertha Broom! Bertha Broom!" When the whole crowd had joined in the chant, Papa turned this way and that, yelling to the fans: "I knew she could do it! I said so right from the start!" And with all the noise, no one, of course, could hear Mama Bear's groans.

Chapter 11
Hail to the Chief

On the sidelines, the cheerleaders mixed with the happy players. Suddenly the loudspeakers crackled again. Bert Brunowski's voice boomed across the playing field.

"May I have your attention, please!"

Coach Grizzmeyer waved his arms for quiet.

"The results of yesterday's election are as follows," said Brunowski. "Queenie McBear, 56. Brother Bear, 56. Mr. Honeycomb will announce tomorrow how the tie will be broken."

Sister Bear shook her head in disgust. "A tie—I knew it!"

"But that can't be!" said Bertha Broom.

"Why not?" Lizzy Bruin asked.

"Because I voted for Brother," said Bertha.

The cheerleaders let out a gasp. "You *what?*" they said.

"I voted for Brother," Bertha repeated.

"But what about your responsibility to all your sisters at Bear Country School?" demanded Queenie.

Bertha draped a heavy arm around Brother's shoulders. "My first responsibility is to my quarterback—both on the field and off."

"Wait a minute," said Freddy. "That means we have to count again. If Bertha voted for Brother, the vote should be 57–55 in favor of Brother!"

"Except for one thing," Skuzz said out of the side of his mouth. "Too-Tall voted for Queenie."

"*Too-Tall voted for Queenie!*" the cubs exclaimed. "*Why?*"

"Very simple," muttered Skuzz, with a mocking glance at his gang leader. "He's crazy about her."

Too-Tall blushed deeply and dug a toe into the turf. "I guess I'm a traitor for love," he mumbled as Queenie leaned over and kissed him on the cheek.

"That Queenie!" whispered Sister to Lizzy. "That's why she wasn't worried about a tie! But she didn't know that Bertha would vote for Brother!"

"So it *is* a tie, after all," said Freddy. "I guess we'll just have to wait until tomorrow to find out what's going to happen."

But Brother Bear already had a good idea of what was going to happen. Now he was more sure than ever that he couldn't possibly be president and help the Bear Country Cousins to a winning football season at the same time. After all, the team had barely won just now, even though he had just played the best game of his life. On top of that, Brother knew how much Queenie wanted to be president. And it didn't seem fair that he should enjoy this moment of football glory and maybe win the election, too.

"We won't have to wait until tomorrow," Brother said, stepping forward. "Tell you what, Queenie. I withdraw. That makes you president of the school."

"You do?" said Queenie with wide-open eyes. "But why?"

Brother shrugged. "I believe in 'ladies first.' "

"Oh, is that so!" cried Lizzy Bruin.

"Queenie," said Sister angrily, "are you going to accept the presidency after a male chauvinist remark like that?"

Queenie looked around the group with a sly smile. "You're darned right I am!" she said.

As things turned out, Queenie made a pretty good president, Brother had a very good year as quarterback, and Bertha Broom proved to be a *heckuva* fullback.

The mystery of who had stolen Bertha's pads remained unsolved for some time. But Too-Tall always had a way of finding these

things out. After the football season was over, he reported that three of the Beartown Bullies had confessed to the crime.

It seems that the idea of being beaten by a girl filled the three players with such terror that they were moved to commit a crime. And that crime was to be remembered in Bear Country as an especially nasty symbol of male chauvinism.

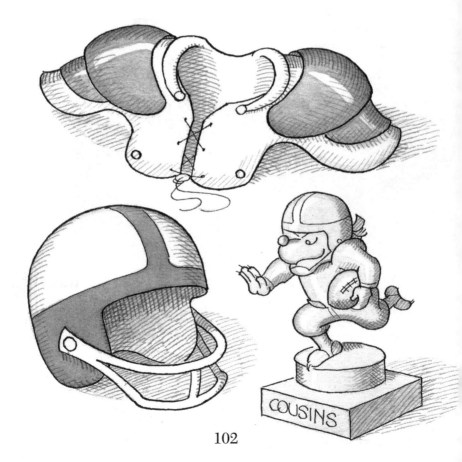

Stan and Jan Berenstain began writing and illustrating books for children in the early 1960s, when their two young sons were beginning to read. That marked the start of the best-selling Berenstain Bears series. Now, with more than 95 books in print, videos, television shows, and even Berenstain Bears attractions at major amusement parks, it's hard to tell where the Bears end and the Berenstains begin!

Stan and Jan make their home in Bucks County, Pennsylvania, near their sons—Leo, a writer, and Michael, an illustrator—who are helping them with Big Chapter Books stories and pictures. They plan on writing and illustrating many more books for children, especially for their four grandchildren, who keep them well in touch with the kids of today.